DINGLE

DOWN THE YEARS

A collection of old photographs
compiled by

TOM FOX

BRANDON

First published in 1992 by Brandon Book Publishers Ltd,
Dingle, Co. Kerry, Ireland.

To Dingle people near and far

British Library Cataloguing in Publication Data is available for this book.

ISBN 0 86322 155 6

Cover design by Paul Dyson
Typeset by Brandon
Printed by Colour Books, Dublin

Contents

Sponsors

Fergus Ó Flaithbheartaigh; Tom O'Donnell; The Dingle Pub; Granville's Siopa Decor; Tommy & Thérèse Devane; The McKenna Family, Dykegate Street; Doyles Seafood Bar & Townhouse; John "Diony" O'Connor, EBS; AIB Bank; Pat & Ger Fox; Con & Angela Mangan, Limerick; Tadhg & Eibhlín Ó Coileáin; Brendan Faherty, Builder; Frank O'Connor & Co, Solicitors; Harringtons Restaurant; John & Colette Ashe; Jimmy & Patsy Fenton; Benners Hotel; Bank of Ireland; Sean O'Sullivan & Co, Chartered Accountants; Flogas Ireland Ltd; Brian de Staic; Meán Scoil na Toirbhirte; Eileen & Gene Courtney; Lord Bakers Seafood Restaurant; Hillgrove Hotel; P. & T. Fitzgerald, Dingle; Padraig Lynch; T.P. Ó Concubhair; R & S Engineering (Dingle) Ltd; Helen & Ita Griffin; Canon Jack McKenna; Peter J. Callery; Half Door Restaurant; Marion Kavanagh; O'Connor's Garage; Bambury's, Mail Road; Pat & Eva Hennessy; J. O'Keefe MPSI; TSB Bank; John & Celeste Slye; Thomas & Kate Ashe; Geaney's Bar; Breandán Ó Murchú, Corcaigh; Paddy Bawn Brosnan's; Dingle Harbour Commissioners.

Introduction by Canon Jack McKenna

The story of human habitation in the Dingle area goes back to pre-history. Ample relics of pre-history – megalithic tombs, promontory forts, ogham stones and ancient churches – abound in the area.

With the coming of the Normans, Dingle developed into one of the most prominent trading centres in the south-west due to their astute craft and business-like attitude. The earliest official references to Dingle in the state papers are in connection with trade through the harbour. In 1257 King Henry III of England imposed a customs duty on goods exported through Dingle. Maurice Fitzgerald, first Earl of Desmond, got sanction from the King to impose another tax on all wines imported through the port. Trade flourished under those early Normans and by the end of the thirteenth century they had exported more goods through Dingle than through the port of Limerick.

According to tradition a Norman family, the Husseys, gave its name to the town. Daingean Uí Chúis is translated as Dingle of the Husseys. Hugh de Hoese, the first of the family to come to Ireland, came over with Maurice Fitzgerald, one of the original invaders of 1169. The Fitzgeralds held the title Earl of Desmond and the Husseys were given land under their Lordship.

Another branch of the Fitzgeralds received the title Knight of Kerry. From 1259 until 1780 the Knights of Kerry held property in Dingle and were the centre of political and social life in the town. The Knight's castle stood where the Temperance Hall and the Post Office now stand. In later years the family lived in a spacious mansion at the top of the Grove until their departure in 1780.

In his book, *Antient and Present State of Kerry* (1756), Charles Smith gives an insight into the Spanish influence in Dingle. He writes: "Several of the houses were built in the Spanish fashion... this place being formerly much frequented by ships of that nation... The parish church, dedicated to St James is said to have been formerly built at the charge of the Spanish" (Pp. 176-77). Charles V, King of Spain and Emperor of the Holy Roman Empire, sent his personal envoy, Gonzalo Fernandez, to Dingle in 1529 to have talks with the Earl of Desmond regarding their respective military activities.

Another prominent Norman family in Dingle was the Rice family, of which James Louis Rice was undoubtedly the most celebrated member. Born in Dingle, he emigrated to the Continent and enlisted in the Irish Brigade in Austria. He reached a position of eminence there and became a personal friend of the Emperor, Joseph II, who created him Count of the Holy Roman Empire. When the French Revolution shook France and the whole of Europe, Count Rice with some trustworthy friends, one of them another Dingle man, Thomas Trant, devised a plan to rescue Marie Antoinette, sister of Joseph II and Queen of France, from her prison in Paris. Dingle was the intended refuge of the Queen and Count Rice had his old home in the town prepared for her. That house is now the office of Údarás na Gaeltachta in Dingle. The plan was unsuccessful.

Dingle was burned during the Desmond wars. In 1585 Queen Elizabeth I, according to the Calendar of Patent Rolls, sanctioned a grant of £300 to enclose Dingle with defence walls. The same document set up the Corporation of Dingle and promised the grant of a charter to the town, which was finalised in 1607 under King James I. Dingle thus became the first town in Kerry to receive a charter. The corporation began to function as from 1585 with its headquarters in the Market House, which stood where P. & T. Fitzgerald's supermarket now stands. The head of the corporation was designated Sovereign of Dingle and was elected annually on 25 July, the Feast of St James, Patron of Spain. It regulated the affairs of Dingle for more than two hundred years, the last Sovereign being John Hickson who lived in the Grove House, former residence of the Knight of Kerry. He was Sovereign for the year 1820.

The middle of the sixteenth century marked the beginning of the linen industry, which shot like a meteor across the history of Dingle. It left folk memories and place names such as the Bleach, Holy Ground, The Linen Hall, to echo that very prosperous period of the economic life of the place. It declined at the beginning of the nineteenth century – the century which brought the black famine to Ireland and to Dingle. This disaster led to the permanent establishment of the workhouse/hospital by the year 1852.

The nineteenth century saw the building of the Roman Catholic church, the schools, the lighthouse, Esk Tower, Hussey's Folly – features of Dingle which run through this book and are still prominent features today.

Introduction by Tom Fox

Old photos were always around our house as long as I remember. They were in albums, in boxes, in books and some were in frames. Those in albums were the real treasures, of course, and were closely guarded by my grandfather, and it was a great treat to be allowed to look at them. The collection was gathered together by his wife Nita and daughter Angela. It was a house that had a lot of contacts. My grandfather, who was a postman in Dingle, was known to everyone locally as was his wife Nita, who worked as a nurse in Dingle Hospital prior to her marriage.

Nita, with Angela's help, kept guests who regularly sent back photos after their visits. All the contacts they had both at home and abroad led to a grand collection of photos. After the death of his wife and daughter my grandfather looked after the photos. When he died in 1980 that job fell to me. Over the last few years I reorganised the albums where necessary and put the ones in boxes into albums. Identification of the photos went on at the same time. In 1985 I took 17 photos for Canon Jack McKenna's history book *Dingle*, and he suggested then that a book of photos of Dingle town should be put together.

In early 1990 I decided to collect together old photos of Dingle town using my own collection as a base. A letter in the *Kerryman* alerted people to my idea. This in itself brought in some photos but the majority of the photos were got by personal calls to local houses and personal letters to people in Ireland, England and America. People were very generous and allowed me in some cases to look through their family albums. I also wrote to institutions. The Department of Irish Folklore in University College Dublin allowed me to search through their vast collection and I came up with many treasures. In many instances people lent me photos on the spot, some came weeks later, more months later.

When I started collecting I was looking for photos for particular sections which I had created: i.e. streets, boats, the pier, trains, processions, etc., but I added new sections as things progressed: sections such as "Dingle Races" and "De Valera in Dingle". I was surprised at the volume of photos of Dingle that existed, and I believe that there are more which did not come to light. The publication of this book will alert people to the importance of the photos they have and hopefully prompt others to search for photos they think they might have.

The majority of photos are in private family collections, mainly collected and kept by the women. Many of the photos which are treasured by their owners are also national treasures. I am very grateful to people for allowing me to use their photos in my book

I hope that you will enjoy looking through this book again and again, reminding yourself of how Dingle looked "down the years".

Tom Fox, The Mall, Dingle
October 1992

Nita Murphy

Angela Fox

Dingle's Oldest Photograph.
Very Rev Patrick A. Griffin 1839-1871.
Ordained in 1865, he spent nine months as a curate in Dingle (1866-67).
He was curate in Ballyferriter from November 1867 to February 1870 and in Causeway
from 1870 to 1871. He was the first priest to be buried in the graveyard adjacent to
St Mary's Church, Green St. The photograph was taken between 1865 and 1871.

Dingle circa 1878-1898. The town clock was installed in 1878 with financial assistance from Lord Ventry. The photo was originally published in 1898. The Royal Irish Constabulary barracks was not built at the time. (photo: J.C. Hyland, Chicago)

Dingle at the turn of the century. The RIC barracks now dominates the scene. Houlihan's power plant is on right hand side of photo.

Dingle 1955. The Garda station stands where the RIC barracks (burned 1922) once stood.
The house under construction is O'Loughlins.

Bridge Street in the '50s. Barry's Forge is the single-storey building.

The Feis in progress in the grounds of the Christian Brothers School. Several platforms were provided to accommodate all the different events. Competitions were held for singing, dancing, recitations etc. It was organised by the townspeople. (1910-20)

The Feis was preceded by a parade around the town. Here it passes the ruin of the RIC barracks. The jerseys read "Clann na Fodhla".

An Seabhac, Padraig Ó Siochrú (front row, sitting tenth from left) with a group
of students from one of the Irish colleges he organised.

After a lapse of many years the Feis
was revived in the '50s. It was
opened by De Valera (see De
Valera in Dingle) and An Seabhac
(seen here) gave the oration of the
Feis. (photo: Murtagh Burke)

The interior of St Mary's Church with its limestone pillars and Gothic arches which stood there for a hundred years until removed in the renovations in 1965. The lights were replaced by Canon Browne after 1929 as were the altar rails with wooden tops.

St Mary's Church.

Dingle Choir, 1900.

Top left: Very Rev Daniel Canon O'Sullivan (Fr Dan) was the man responsible for the building of the church 1862-65. He was parish priest from 1856-1898.

Top right: Very Rev John Canon McDonnell, parish priest from 1919-29.

Bottom left: Very Rev Thomas Canon Lyne, parish priest from 1936-1961. (photo: Murtagh Burke)

Fr Tom and Fr Jack.

Padraig Lynch, who is parish clerk since 1942.

First Communion group in Green St.

Grotto of Our Lady of Fatima.

With the roof removed the organ loft
is visible. (photo: Jack McKenna)

Scaffolding surrounds the sanctury during rebuilding in 1965.
(photo: Jack McKenna)

The Blessed Sacrament, under cover and with a guard of honour,
leads the procession through Bridge Street. (1910-20)

Procession in Green St 1923. The sides of the street were lined with bushes and
trees especially for the occasion.

The Boy Scouts provide a guard of honour for the altar boys carrying the crucifix and candles. They are followed by the children who precede the adults. Banners are prominent as the procession comes down Main St.

The procession turns the corner from The Mall into Bridge St.

Young girls in their First Communion outfits parade past the old post office in Strand St. The buntings were erected especially for the procession.

Margaret Kennedy (Mag the Fish) dressed up in her best for the procession. She proudly wears her sodality medal. The window of Fox's, The Mall is specially prepared for the procession with statue and flowers. Rex the dog sits patiently nearby.

Procession passes through Holy Ground. The army provide a guard of honour.

The men parade down Main St on two separate occasions.

Arrival of 11.45 Mail at Dingle Train Station. (1910-1920)

Officials of Dingle train (left to right):
Johnny O'Connor, (unknown), Tom Bailey, Station Master.

Left: Jim Sullivan, railway guard, with his wife Mary Ann.

Below: Three railway wagons at Strand St, 1899. The track extended to the root of the pier at that time. (photo: John Willis, Wales)

Loco No. 1T with empty cattle trucks, 24-7-51. (photo: P.C. Allen)

Loco No. 2T on a fair day, 26-7-52 at cattle dock. (photo: D.G. Rowlands)

Top: The Dingle train, under full steam, heads out the Mail Road to Tralee.

Left: A horse-drawn caravan passes by the railway tracks that ran to the pier.

Above: Railway sign at Ballinasteenig just outside Dingle. Molly Sullivan in front.

Right: Small Mickey Moriarty, engine driver, 1933.

Below: Train crew and road freight crew (late 1950s). Left to right: T. Hourigan (fireman), Billy O'Hanlon (loco driver), Thade Nolan (steamriser), Eddie Clancy (road freight department), Jimmy "Slim" Foley (guard), Willie Curtin (fireman), Tom Flaherty (road freight department).

Dingle station in the early 1950s getting ready for the monthly cattle train.

Loco No. 1T in Dingle, July 1951. The monthly cattle special. This is the engine (repaired) which 58 years earlier had toppled over Curraduff viaduct, Camp, killing 3 people and about 90 pigs. (photo: Walter McGrath)

CIE staff 1953.
Inspector Crowe, O'Connor, Lynch, Paddy Kennedy, Paddy McWilliams (photo: D.G. Rowlands).

Daisies growing up through the tracks signify the end of the line. This photo was taken in Tralee before the last "special" run of the train. Left to right: Mr Garvey (Station Master, Tralee), Mr Garrett (Tralee Loco Super), H.A. Massey (Cork Loco Super), Willie Lynch (Fireman), Bill O'Hanlon (Driver).

Right: Royal Irish Constabulary barracks which dominated The Mall in its time.

Below: Ginders, Major Browne and another few Dingle Black & Tans, 1919/20.

Hudson's Bridge and The Mall. RIC barracks is on the left and CBS on right.

Left: Boys and girls gather outside Duckhams, The Mall. Kitty Duckham had a draper's shop here. The blinds were drawn on a sunny day to protect the merchandise from sunlight.

Below: Ashes' truck, fully laden, ready for deliveries. Ashes were the Guinness agents and also bottled their own minerals.

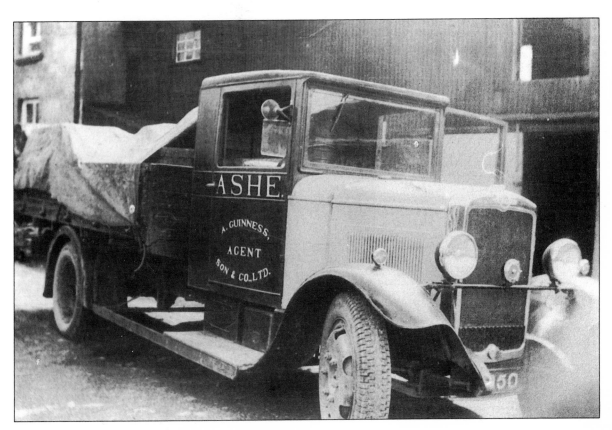

Left: Mag the Fish. Mag bought fish from the fishing boats and then sold it to the householders. She used a dish to carry the fish. She normally went around barefooted.

Below: Group at top of Mall. Left to right: Ned Dowd, John Spillane, Timmy McMahon, Johnny Martin, Pat McLoughlin.

Garda station and The Mall. (1950s)

Group outside Garda Station. Left to right: Tadgh Kavanagh, garda, Johnny Moriarty,
Gallerus, Kruger Kavanagh, garda, Joe Foley in front, (unknown behind), (unknown),
Brendan Kavanagh, Murreagh. (1943)

St John's Well, which was situated at The Mall. Rounds were made annually to
this well on 8 September.

Mick O'Connor, The Mall (2nd from right) delivers visitors to Dunquin.
Robin Flower on right.

The door of Fox's boarding house/guest house. Left to right: Billy Murdoch, Angela Fox, Andy Higgins, Lily Gould.

Burnham House, residence of Lord Ventry. After the First World War he sold it to the Land Commission. The Department of Education acquired it at a later date. The Order of Mercy turned it into a boarding school and gave it the title Coláiste Íde.

Lord Ventry's staff.

Lord Ventry's tea party was held anually for the children of his staff.

Barry's Forge and house at Holy Ground. The pole for bending the iron banding into circles is right of centre. An entrance to the Garda Station is on right hand side. (photo: Caoimhín Ó Danachair)

Group outside the forge, 1930's. Back row left to right: Mikey Fitz, John St; Paud Shea; Danny Flahive; Tommy Barry; Sean Barry. Front row left to right: Henry Shea, John Martin.

Barracks yard, 1927. Left to right, back: Jack Connor, Kevin Barry, Eamon Connor, Thomas McKenna, Tom Devane, Paddy Devane, Michael Moore, Paddy Joe Flaherty, Jimmy Flahive, George Graham. Middle row: Jimmy Shea, John Boland, John "Shine" Long, Michael Devane, Michael Shea, Tom Long. Front: John Deváne, Dermot Graham, Paddy Devane, Eugene O'Connor, Pat McCarthy, Michael Boland.

Group left to right, back: John Flaherty, (unknown), Kathleen O'Connor, Paddy Bawn Brosnan, Noreen Murphy, Michael McCarthy, Tim Brosnan, Tommy Brosnan, (unknown), Patrick Flaherty, Paddy Flannery, Paddy Bowler. Middle: Colm Lynch,, Jimmy Bowler, Mickie Callaghan, John Joe Flannery, Tom Flannery, Kevin Lynch, Tommy Joe Curran, Eddie Moore, Brendan Bowler, George Flaherty, Tomáisín Flannery. Front: Michael Begley.

Jamie Martin (top) and Eilish Shea (below)

Willie Long, harness maker, at work in his premises in Holy Ground.

Mike Shea putting the finishing touches to a cart which he hand-made. His wife ran a sweet shop as did Moriartys next door.

Mick Boland putting the finishing touches to a cart wheel before the metal band is applied. The stock (centre piece) of the wheel is elm, the spokes are oak and the fellows (outer rim) are also of elm. (photo: George Twist) 1966

Presentation nuns at Our Lady's Grotto.

Group outside cookery room, 1930s

1. Kathleen Sullivan, Ballinasig; 2. Hannah Manning; 3. Dora O'Connor, Ballinasig; 4. Mary Slattery, Cottages; 5. Shea, Comeen; 6. Hannah Shea, Holy Ground; 7. Eileen Flaherty, Grey's Lane; 8. Bridie Devane; 9. Mercy Scanlon; 10. Georgina O'Connor, Ventry; 11. Noreen O'Donnell; 12. Ellen Farrell; 13. Hannah Kennedy, Doonshean; 14. Kathleen Sullivan, Ballyhea; 15. Rita Flaherty, Grey's Lane; 16. Eileen Connor (The Post); 17. Eileen Sheehy, Grey's Lane; 18. Bridie Casey, Ballinclár; 19. Rose Slattery, The Cottages; 20. Daisy O'Connell; 21. Nora Sheehy, Glens; 22. Kitty Long; 23. Mercy Scanlon, Sráidbhaile; 24. Mary Russell; 25 Teresa Flahive, The Quay; 26. Eileen Johnson; 27. Sheila McCarthy; 28. Catherine Devane; 29. Mary Landers, Knockavrogeen; 30. Hanora Kennedy; 31. Bridie Sullivan; 32. Maureen Brosnan; 33. Kathleen Connor.

Fourth class in the convent. Sr Berthmanns was the teacher. (*c.* 1927)

Front (left to right): Josephine Connor, Garraí; Hannah Shea, Holy Ground; Eileen Lynch, Kilfountain; Josie Quill, Goat Street; Hannie Connor, Green Street; Mary Moore, Grey's Lane. 2nd row: Pattie Murdoch, Green Street; Mary Ashe, The Mall; Eileen Fox, Monaree; Eileen Martin, John Street; Hannah Foley, Inch; Mary Galvin, John Street; Teresa Connor, John Street. 3rd row: Cristina Connor, Ballinasig; Nonie Hehir, Goat Street; Nellie Quirke, Dykegate Street; Mary Flaherty, Grey's Lane; Nonie Reynolds, Colony; Kathy Dady, Colony; Katie Walsh, Milltown. 4th row: Bridgie Kennedy, John Street; Maureen Kavanagh, Burnham; Nellie Quirke, Dykegate Street; Mary B. Sullivan, Knockavrogeen; Bridie Donnelly, Dykegate Street; Kathleen McCarthy, Burnham. Back row: Katie Kenny, Goat Street; Nonie Kennedy, Garfinny; Katie Dady, Milltown; Gertie Thomas, Goat Street; Mary Lyne, Burnham; Cecila Devane, The Station; Kathleen Rayel, Beenbawn.

Above: Shamrock
Wren passes ruins of
RIC barracks. (1928)

Right: Wren in
Strand St, 1928.

Below: The
hobbyhorse, a feature
of the wren in Dingle,
16/12/34.

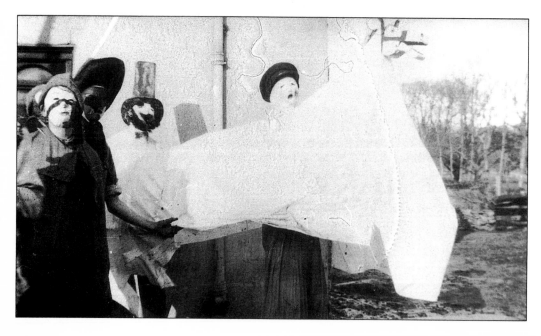

Great effort was spent on creating a rig for the wren, as can be seen here. Potatoes and a carrot make up the necklace; the headgear and dress are cabbage leaves.

Little Boy Blue, Fred and Ginger refers to Fred Astaire and Ginger Rogers, two of Hollywood's stars.

Most wrens had a stunt which reflected topical issues of the times. The captured airman (above) and the aeroplane (below) could refer to the Mount Brandon air crashes during World War II.

The Great White Hope, from the era of Joe Louis, the great American boxer.
Taking the part is Johnny "eat a bite" Kennedy who lived in Mikey Casey's,
John Street. Joe Louis, a black man, dominated boxing so much that boxing
promoters started looking for the "great white hope" that would defeat him.

Banner reads "making a living".

Favourite for the Grand National 1934 could refer to Golden Miller who won
the Gold Cup in 1934, '35, '36. He fell both times he entered the Grand National.

The Main Street Wren.

Fighting Sanctions refers to sanctions against Mussolini.

The Goat Street Wren. Seanín Scanlon, Chapel Lane, holds the banner.
Jimmy Quirke and Sean Scanlon, Chapel Lane, are unmasked on the right.

Goat Street Wren with stunt on donkey-drawn cart.

The Quay Wren.

Stunt for the Goat Street Wren 1938 at Falvey's Market Field. Dingle had won the County Football Championship for the first time. Figures represented are Sean Brosnan and Bill Dillon. Left to right: Anton Curran, Jimmy Broadhurst, Dinny, Jimmy Falvey, Jack Harris, Patrick Cronesbury, Paddy Lynch. (photo: Mikey Quirke)

Wren boy at Foxy John's door, 1963. (photo: Lisa Stephens)

Wren boys at Strand Street, 1963. (photo: Lisa Stephens)

Above: De Valera arriving at the top of the Mall to address the assembled crowd. He was in Dingle to support a local candidate in the forthcoming election, 1948. (photo: *Irish Press*)

Left: De Valera in Strand Street in the '50s.

De Valera in Dingle sports field in the '50s. He came to open the Feis which had just been revived. (photo: Murtagh Burke)

De Valera, Tommy Devane and Richard Mulcahy at Dingle sports field, 1967.

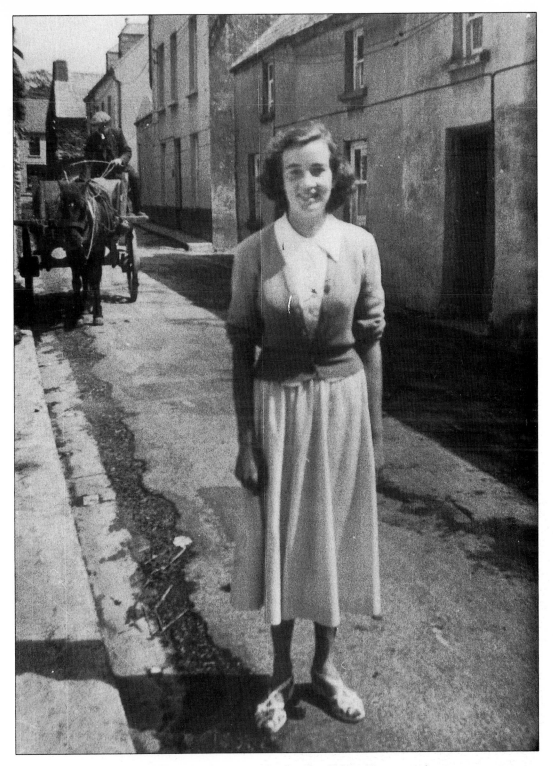

Evelyn Maguire in Dykegate Street. Traditional horse and cart
in background. (photo: Barry Kennedy)

John Street (foreground) and Dingle as viewed from Greenmount. The RIC barracks (left of centre) and the mill at Milltown (background, left) are clearly visible.

Workers dig up the road to lay pipes for the water supply to houses in John Street.

Members of O'Connor family, John Street.

Horse fair at John Street.

The Christian Brothers Monastery and school which was built in a very prominent position.
The foundation stone was laid in 1873.

Busy students experiment in the science laboratory.

Christian Brothers School 1930

Front row, left to right: — Griffin, Paddy Flannery, John Devane, — Quirke, Pat Begley, Thomas O'Donnell, Ml. Kennedy, Jonathan Moriarty, Brendan O'Connor, Timmy Brosnan. Second row: John Rayel, Pat Kennedy, James McCarthy, Ml. Lynch, Ed. Rayel, Patrick Begley, Anthony Manning, Pat Lovett, James O'Connor, John Lynch, John (Dixon) Moriarty, John Foley, Thomas Moriarty, Mossy Moore. Third row: Michael Galvin, Eamon O'Connor, John McKenna, John Moriarty, Paddy Barrett, John O'Donoghue, Billy Murdoch, Tommy Kevane, Michael Barrett, Michael O'Donoghue, Alex. O'Donnell, Paddy C. Brosnan. Fourth row: Tom McKenna, Johnny McKenna, James Farrell, Patrick Lynch, Tom Long, Seán Sugrue, Louis Graham, Michael Ferriter, — O'Connor, John Kelliher, Ml. Kennedy, James Quinn, Rev Br O'Mahony. Back row: Rev Br Long, Michael Lovett, Cornelius Brosnan, Ml. Houlihan, P. Kenny, John Griffin, Ed. Foley, Micheál Devane, Gerald Griffin, — Hehir.

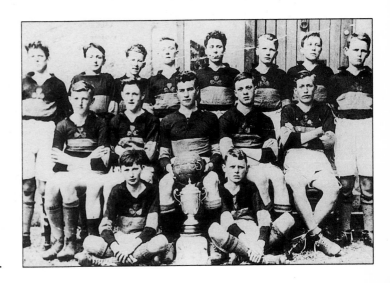

School Team, 1934/35.

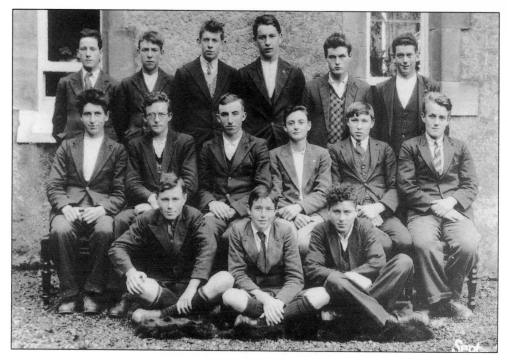

Class of 1934 left to right back row: (unknown), (unknown), (unknown), (unknown), Joe Fitz, (unknown). Middle: Denis Brosnan, Foxy John Moriarty, Mike Falvey, Joe Adams, Danny Murphy, Gerald Fox. Front: Tom Flaherty, Mickie Quirke, Gega Connor.

The best all-Irish speaking school in 1940. Seamus O'Halloran accepts the shield from Tadhg O'Tuama, Cigire. Tom Lundon, teacher, looks on from the left as does Brother Ryan, headmaster, Canon Lyne and Sean Brosnan (all on right).

Houses in Green Street (left to right): McCarthy's (worked in creamery), Katie Sarah Griffin's shop, Bridget "Bullseye" Murphy's shop, Murdocks. (photo: Carl Von Sydow, *c.* 1925)

Carved stones in houses in Green Street, 1947. (photos: Caoimhín Ó Danachair)

Above: Houses in Green Street. On the left are Tom Connor's, Tom Sullivan's, Paddy Garry's and Moore's, victualler.

Right: Harness maker in Green Street (O'Connors).

Left: Woman with traditional shawl in Green Street.

Below: The well-tended garden of the Presbytery in Green Street. St Mary's Church dominates the background and the Presentation Convent is on the right.

Right: Katie Sarah Griffin's shop in Green Street, 1947. (photo: Caoimhín Ó Danachair)

Below: Group of children in Green Street.

Green Street with Munster & Leinster Bank on right.

Lower Green Street.

Above: Family of Patrick and Margaret Devane (Disette). Standing (left to right): Michael (Dr), Sheila (Gunning), Molly. Sitting: Rita, Kathleen (Stack), Jack, Josephine (Cullen). Paddy (left) became the main fish processor and exporter in Dingle in the '30s and '40s.

Eileen Malone and Noreen Curran.

John Mitchell and Michael Lovett at corner of Holy Ground and Green Street. (photo: Murtagh Burke)

On Sunday afternoons Dingle people went to their favourite spots. A walk around Cooleen to the lookout post near the coastguard station, out along the Banks to Hussey's Folly, the lighthouse, Sláidín and on to Nancy Brown's Parlour for a paddle. The daring would head for the pier and borrow one of the punts belonging to the fishing fleet and row around the harbour, often heading for the broken bridge (below) at Burnham. Burnham Hill, Greenmount and Cnoc a' Cairn, which give the best views of Dingle, were often climbed on Sundays.

Punt inside broken bridge at Burnham. Gerald Fox at the helm; Angela Fox, second from left.

Old and young taking it easy. The hats, waistcoats and long stockings were the style of the times.

At the coastguard station are (back, left to right) Johnny McKenna, Tommy Devane, Tom Long; front: Kevin Barry (the Forge).

The cairn on Cnoc a' Cairn which was built in the '30s, some say as a monument to the dole.

Esk Tower, Burnham, erected in 1847 to guide ships and boats into Dingle Harbour.

Dingle lighthouse, which was built in 1886-87.
Tadhgin Galvin on left.

Hussey's Folly was built in the 1840s by a grant from
Edward Hussey to give relief to a famine-stricken people.

Right: John Joe Fox relaxing in a punt. Construction of "open eye" extension is progressing in the background.

Below: Mike Ryle and Tomás Shea, Holy Ground. Both worked in Atkins'.

Michael Long, Bill Barry and Jim McKenna taking it easy near the Conor Pass. 12 May 1949
(photo: Murtagh Burke)

The Union Workhouse dominates the scene as viewed from Cnoc a' Cairn.

Michael O'Sullivan outside his premises. A firkin of butter can be seen in the cart.

Above: John Long and his wife
Mary.

Left: A billhead of John Long's.

Left: Mikey Grandfield, Nell's father.

Below: Nell Grandfield at the doorway of her sweetshop in Strand Street.

Griffin Family, Strand Street, 1898. Back, left to right: Nellie, Patrick, Andrew, James, Timothy (Tadhg). Front: Mary, Mayme, James A., Margaret.

Donkeys and carts with milk churns head for the creamery. (photo: P.C. Allen)

Taking it easy at root of pier. Weighbridge in background.

The Garraí in the early '30s. The house with the *Irish Press* sign had the first franchise for selling newspapers in Dingle.

Strand Street with the old post office on the right and the Red Shed in the background.

Below left: The Red Shed was blown down in a storm on the night of 26 December 1951. Below right is a view of the storm damage at the root of the pier. Pats Brosnan is on the left. (photos: M. Burke)

Above left: Mike Long, Eugene Brosnan and Lisa Moriarty inside her shop. (photo: Lisa Stephens 1963)

Above right: Jonathan Moriarty in his shop. (photo: Lisa Stephens 1963)

Left: Maurice Lynch, tailor.

Above: Assembled for a day's sport with the beagles. Diony O'Connor (8th from left) and Bill Dillon (4th from right).

Left: Mike Fox, fisherman, with his beagle.

Tommy Ashe, The Quay, holding the banner of the Dingle Boy Scout Brigade. Anthony O'Connor (right) was the scout master. Tommy died 21 March 1935 aged 15.

Original caption reads "Ten minutes, Pat", which indicates that Paddy Long, who became a Christian Brother, had a time limit in which to chop the wood. John O'Donnell keeps a watch.

Dingle Boy Scout Brigade, established 1932 by Fr Hurley.

Tending the camp fire under the watchful eye of scoutmaster Anthony O'Connor;
(bottom right) Johnín Sullivan with mug in hand.

Scout masters: on left Jack McKenna and Gerald Keane; on right Anthony
O'Connor. Boy Scouts, front row, left to right: Thomas Moriarty, Timmy
Sullivan, (unknown), Johnny McKenna (Holy Ground), Gega Connor, Paud
O'Shea. Back row, left to right: Louis Graham, Paddy Long, Michael Murphy,
(unknown), Tommy Devane, (unknown).

Girl guides, established after 1932. Front, left to right: Kath Galvin, Hilda
Moriarty, May Dillon, Fr Hurley, Eileen Cremin, Angela Long, Teresa
Moriarty. Middle: May Devane, (unknown), Gertie Thomas, Kathy
O'Connor, Rita Graham, Mary Galvin, (unknown), — Graham (Avondale).
Back row: Kath McKenna, — Foley (Inch), Bridie O'Sullivan, Mary Graham
(Cooleen).

Girl Guide Committee; left to right: May Duckham, Mrs Dr O'Donnell,
Mrs Ashe, Quay, Mrs Dr Murphy, Kit O'Donnell, May O'Sullivan.

Girl Guides, 1936 (left to right): Kathy McKenna, Rita Graham, Eileen T. O'Connor,
May Sullivan, Kathy O'Connor, Bridie Sullivan.

Dingle Rugby Team, 1912. Paddy Devane middle row second from left.

Dingle Rugby Team, 1928/29. Back row, left to right: Fitzgerald, Joe
Guiheen, Murphy (Sea field), Maurice Moriarty, Burke, Dr Scully,
(unknown), Tom McKenna. Front: Dick MacDonald, Tomas Kavanagh,
Owens, John Moore, Mulverhill, Jack Connor, Carney. Sitting: Paddy
Guiheen, Tommy Nelligan.

Above: Dingle Golf Club, Ballintaggart. Back row, left to right: Bill Murdock, Galvin, Dick MacDonald, (unknown), Paddy Ryle, Tommy Ryle, Dr O'Donnell, Mike Ryle, Tommy Nelligan, Tommy Duckham. Middle row: Wilson, Mrs Dr Murphy, Mrs Dr O'Donnell, Mrs Wilson, Una Murdock, Harry Meek. Front: Nellie Nelligan, Kathleen O'Donnell. Two caddies at side are Mickey Callaghan (with clubs) and Willie Slattery.

Left: Big Jim Ashe playing golf at Doonsheen.

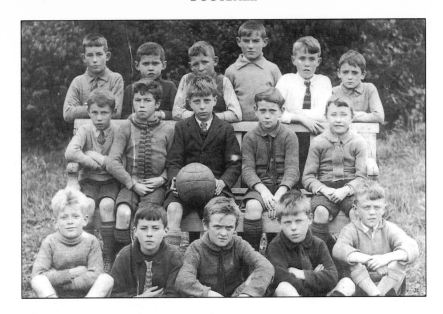

Street Team, 1926. Back row, left to right: Bill Dillon, Tommy
Kennedy, Jimmy Barry, Eugene Connor, Gerald Fox, Luke Ferriter.
Middle row: James Barrett, Mossy Quirke, John Gould, Jermiah
Sullivan, Desmond O'Connor. Front: Jimmy Lawlor, Mikey Sheehy,
John Sullivan, Patrick Brosnan, Michael Reen.

Quay Team, 1928. Back row, left to right: Johnny Callaghan, Tommy
Brosnan, Jack Flaherty, Jim Long, John Joe Sheehy, Tomás Shea, Joe
Flaherty, John Devane, Mike Shea, Jackie Graham. Front row: Mickey
Flannery, Johnny Browne, Dutch Flannery (capt), Jimmy McKenna, Joe
Shea (ball boy), Mick Boland, Christy Hurley, John Long (Tom's brother),
Johnny Flannery. Boy at side: Mikey Callaghan.

Dingle CBS, Dunloe Cup Winners 1928. Back row, left to right: Rev Bro Ryan, J. Long RIA, J. Connor, G. Graham, M. McKenna, P. Devane, J. Dillon. Middle: J.A. O'Connor, M. Cleary, M. Shea (capt), M. Devane, J. Fitzgerald, J. Sullivan. Front: T. Falvey, T. O'Connor, J. Shea, P. Devane.

Dingle County Champions, 1938. Front, on ground, left to right: Mossy Moore, Jimmy McCarthy, Tommy Devane, Jack McKenna. Front row, seated: Ned Kennedy, Willie Casey, Tim Brosnan, Sean Brosnan, Very Rev Canon Lyne, James McKenna (capt) Brother Grennan, Gerald Fox, Tommy O'Sullivan, Paddy Barrett, Tom O'Connor. Standing: Michael O'Donoghue (sec), Michael O'Shea (treas) Jackie Sullivan (chairman), Mikey Callaghan, Patrick O'Donoghue, Johnny Moriarty, Paddy Bawn Brosnan, Tom Long, Bill Dillon, Michael O'Flaherty, John Moriarty, Paddy Devane, Danny McCarthy, Bill O'Connor (trainer). Back row: Tadhg Kavanagh, Paddy Bowler, Paddy Kennedy, Tom O'Sullivan, Jim Ashe, Mike Kennedy, Mick Boland, Mikey O'Shea, Tommy McCarthy, Pat McCarthy, Harry Meeke, Jim G. Ashe.

Dingle County Champions, 1941 and 1943. On ground: Jack McKenna, Mossy Moore.
Front row: Tom Flaherty, Paddy Bawn Brosnan, Canon Lyne, Fr Beasley, Br Doherty, Johnny
O'Connor (the post). Second row: Tommy Sullivan, Patrick Cronesbury, Bill Casey, J. Sayers, John
(Dixon) Moriarty, Barty Garvey, Tom Long, Gerald Fox. Back row: John Brosnan, Mikey Donoghue,
Johnny Barrett, Denis Drake, Danny McCarthy, John Joe Fox. Inset: Johnny Moriarty, Bill Dillon, Gega
O'Connor, Paddy Barrett, Bill Connor, Diony O'Connor, Tim Brosnan, Sean Brosnan, Michael
O'Leary, Christy Murphy, Gerald Teehan.

1941 Team: M. Moore, T. Barrett, P.B. Brosnan, T. Brosnan, T. O'Sullivan, W. Casey, P. Cronesbury,
T. Flaherty, S. Brosnan, W. Dillon, T. O'Connor (capt), Dixon Moriarty, T. Long, C. Murphy, J.
Moriarty.

Dingle County Champions, 1940. Back row, left to right: Paddy Donoghue, Jimmy Connor, Tom Devane, Paddy Devane, (unknown), Mikey Donoghue, Mick Dowd. Standing: Danny McCarthy, Patrick Cronesbury, Joe Fitz, Vincent Betts, Michael Ferriter, Tim Brosnan, Michael Sullivan, Gerald Fox, John Moriarty, John Sullivan, Jimmy McKenna, Paddy Bowler, Pat McCarthy in front of Paddy Bowler. Seated: Bill O'Connor, Paddy Bawn Brosnan, Canon Lyne, Tommy Sullivan, Bill Dillon, Fr Jimmy McCarthy, Paddy Barrett, Bill Casey, Joe Shea. In front: Jack McKenna, Tom Long, Mike Devane, Mossy Moore, Tommy Devane.

Dingle County Champions, 1948. Back row, left to right: T. O'Connor, J. Sullivan, Bill Dillon, Billy Casey, T. Flaherty, Paddy Bawn Brosnan, J. Fitzgerald, L. Connor. Front: Thomas Ashe, T. Brosnan, P. Sheehy, Tom Long (capt), E. Fitzgerald, Diony Connor, Tom Sheehy.

Trustees of Dingle Sportsfield. Back row, left to right: Mikey Donoghue, Jimmy Ashe, Jimmy McKenna, John Joe Fox, Pat Sullivan. Front row: Ger Murphy, Dr Scully, Canon Lyne, Father Beasley, Tommy McCarthy, John M. O'Connor.

Three cups in Dingle. Left to right: Munster Cup, Jerry O'Leary with Sam Maguire Cup and John Sullivan, Holy Ground, with County Championship Cup.

Fr Jack McKenna, Tom Long, Bill Dillon and Jimmy McKenna after
County Championship win in 1948.

John Street Social, 1962. Minor Champions. Front row, left to right: Morris Lynch, Michael
Ashe, John Foley, Tommy Devane, Bro Hannon, Mike Sayers, Billy Dillon. Middle row: Joe
Sayers, (unknown), James O'Shea, Bob Sullivan, Michael Sullivan, Fergus Fitzgerald, Pat
Nelligan, Peter Lamb, Leo Brosnan. Back row: James Walsh, Frankie Hanlon, T.P. Ó
Concubhair, (unknown), Paddy Sayers.

On the way to Croke Park 1953.
Back row, left to right: Stevie Kelliher, Tomáisín Lynch, Paddy Flannery, Ger Flahive, John Devane, Eugene Brosnan, Patrick Connor. Front: Timmy Griffin, Gerald Fox.

Houses in Goat Street (right to left): Tom Ashe and his wife Amy Stack, John Kenny (Gobi), Michael Quill, Pats Maguire and his wife Maime Devane, Jimmy Broadhurst, Paddy the Sailor Scanlon. (photo: Carl Von Sydow, *c.* 1925)

Group at Upper Main Street. Back: Luke Fenton. Front, left to right: Hannah Agnes O'Connor, Kathy O'Connor, Margaret O'Connor, Eileen Ferriter.

Fair Day at the Mail Road, circa 1920.

Pig Fair in Main Street.

Pigs in Goat Street, 1963. (photo: Lisa Stephens)

Typical fair day scene at the Mall. (photo: P.C. Allen)

Horses for sale. (photo: P.C. Allen)

Main St and the Bridge area during the fair. (photo: P.C. Allen)

A well-tended flock at the Mall. (photo: P.C. Allen)

Sheep fair in Main Street and John Street. (photo: P.C. Allen)

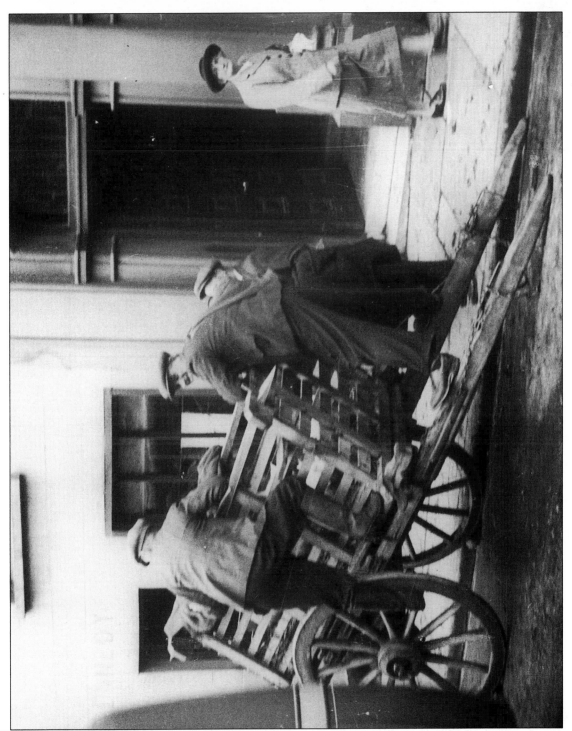

A good sense of balance was a great attribute on a fair day in Main Street. (photo: P.C. Allen)

The sheep fair at Upper Main Street. Stalls selling clothing line the side of the Street. (photo: George Twist 1963)

Pig, five pounds each, 25/8/51. (photo: P.C. Allen)

Peadar Curran at annual horse fair.

A bargain at the price. Market field, Spa Road, 1963. (photo: Lisa Stephens)

Pig fair, Main Street, 1963. Morris Quinn, Curragraig (on left) chatting with a colleague. (photo: Lisa Stephens)

Dingle Brass Band, 1888. Band master Francis Cassidy. Names and instruments (left to right standing): Johnny Walsh, Dykegate Street, Baritone; Andy Houlihan, Upper Main Street, Bombardon; Johnny Deady, Dykegate Street, Baritone; Thomas Moriarty, Dykegate Street, Trombone; Denis McCarthy, Upper Main Street, French Horn; Tom Flynn, Main Street, Euphonium; James Malone, Lough, Clarinet. Sitting: Richard Thomas, Upper Main Street, Side Drum; John Moriarty, Strand Street, Clarinet; John McKenna, Dykegate Street, Clarinet; John O'Connor, Main Street, Cornet; Jim Herlihy, Aunascaul, Big Drum; Jim Deady, Dykegate Street, Cornet; Sean Gould, Upper Main Street, Cornet; Jerry O'Connor, John Street, Cornet; Patrick O'Shea, Main Street, Cornet. Kneeling: James Griffin, Main Street, Cornet. Front: Maurice McKenna Dykegate Street, Sax Horn; John O'Shea, Main Street, Sax Horn; Patrick Walsh, Dykegate Street, Sax Horn. (photo: Mr D'Arcy)

Goat Street Band (left to right): Humphrey Kennedy, Francie Guiheen (Big Drum), Borgie Flaherty, Michael Flannery, Johnny Flannery, Charlie Flannery.

CBS band at Blessing of the Boats.

Goat Street band on pier for Blessing of the Boats. Front row, left to right: Francis Flaherty, Ned Foley, Martin Flannery, Laurence Flannery, Tom Flannery with flag, Anton Connor on the big drum.

Dingle CBS Band 1958.

Front row (left to right): Thomas Moran, Michael Begley, Thomas Ryle, John Hanlon, Michael O'Sullivan, Pat Nelligan, Bob O'Sullivan, James Walsh, Tommy McDonnell. Second row: Fergus Fitzgerald, Patrick Sheehy, Denis O'Leary, Michael McNamara, Michael O'Leary, Jimmy Flannery, Danny Scanlon, Rory O'Connor. Third row: Raymond Scanlon, Peter O'Leary, P.J. Fitzgerald, Tommy McCarthy, John Dillon, John O'Sullivan. Back row: Pat Cashman, Billy Dillon, John Moriarty.

Above: Mike Connor's (Grey's Lane) side car laden for the Dingle Races. On board are (left to right) Cait Donoghue, Mary Tilbury, Margaret Ferriter, Madge Donoghue, Hannah Flaherty. (photo: Owen Curly)

Left: Races Poster, 1933.

The Committee went to Tralee fundraising for the races and ended up in Daly's studio where this photo was taken. Back, left to right: John Malone, Willie Long. Front: Ger Gould, Tomás Kavanagh.

Tommy Duckam, John Malone, Willie Long, Bob Ashe (capt), Dr O'Donnell, James G. Ashe, Father Wolfe (racehorse owner), Higginbotham, six visitors, John Wolfe, Paddy Devane. Middle row: Mikey Ryle, Jack Foley. Front: Danny Griffin, visitor, Tommy Ryle, Reardon, Paddy Ryle, Mick Curran.

Dancing platform, at the Dingle Races, which was organised by Mrs Casey, John Street.

A large crowd at Dingle Races in Ballintaggart. The large covered area was for refreshments.

A line of butter churns on the cobblestones outside Atkins' general store in Main Street. (1910)

The scene at the top of Main Street at the turn of the century. Biddy Dowd, fishseller,
is in the bottom right-hand corner.

Another view of Main Street.

Locals watch as RIC supervise the eviction of the Spanish House – corner of Main Street and Green Street. 1903.

Above: Mowing machine going to Burnham College from Curran's, Main Street. Jim Garvey on machine. The mule and cart, centre right, is from Dunquin. The college horse is on the right. Cart in background belongs to Ned Moran, John Street, street contractor who patched and cleaned the streets. (photo: James Curran 1926)

Right: The Protestant Church (built 1807) as seen from the back of Benner's Hotel. The top of the tower was removed in 1974 as it was in a dangerous condition.

Lee's Hotel, Main Street, housed Dingle's Post Office before it transferred to Strand Street. The hotel was taken over by the Provincial Bank which was amalgamated into Allied Irish Banks.

Rebuilding of the Spanish House. The slogan on the scaffolding reads "O Liberty what crimes are committed in thy name".

A horse and cart, laden with pigs, on the cobblestones of Main Street. (photo: Mason)

Kennedy's, Main Street, now Ashe's Pub.

Group in Main Street, left to right: Paddy Bowler, Maud Griffin, Tom Flaherty, Paddy Kennedy (with cap), Michael Griffin (young boy), (unknown), Bride Moriarty, two young girls, Jack Begley (hands crossed), Tom Hickey, Bill Riley, Tom Moriarty, Jo Griffin, Jimmy McKenna, Maggie Moriarty, Big Jim Ashe, Jack Kennedy, Jamsy Moriarty and Ned Fitzgerald.

May Delia and John Nelligan in their craft shop. (photo: George Twist)

Big Jim Ashe with Bedford truck laden with barrels of porter ready for delivery.

Joe Foley, postman; Hannah Ashe, Jim Ashe, Jack Kennedy.

Above: Mrs Benner (front) in the garden with visitors. She managed Benner's Hotel.

Left: Tom Lundon, a teacher in the CBS for many years, with Peig Sayers. Peig, author of a book of the same name, worked as a *cailín aimsire* in Curran's Main Street for many years. She spent the last years of her life in Dingle hospital.

Main Street in the 1950s.

Main Street. Phelan's Hotel is on the left.

Gerald (Garrett) Fox, postman, empties the box in Main Street.

Gregory Peck with members of the Ashe and McKenna families, 1968.

Mary Curran in her shop in Main Street. (photo: Lisa Stephens 1963)

Transport to Heaven. Jimmy Falvey, Goat Street with his majestic hearse
and elegant team of horses.

Paddy McWilliams standing beside Paddy Baker's car.

Left: Agnes Sheehy, Mary Casey, Kathleen Casey.

Below: Jack Brosnan on his BSA motorbike.

Left: Dingle town's first car, owned by J.C. Houlihan.

Below: Jimmy Falvey with his horse and cart.

Right: Mick Counihan and Bill Dillon with the Dingle Bus.

Below: Junior transport. Tom & Pat Fox.

Carts laden with milk churns line up at Dingle Creamery.

Right: Johnny Lynch, Greenmount at the creamery.

Below: Nationalist fervour expresses itself in this St Patrick's Day parade in the Fair Field, Spa Road.

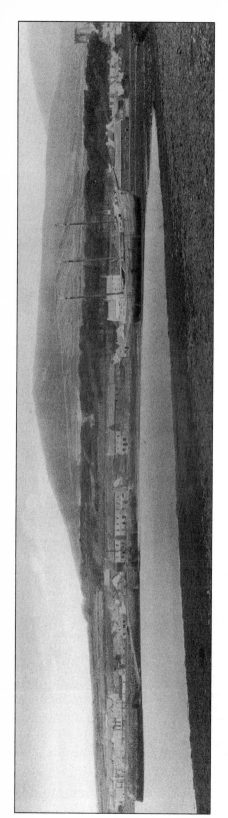

Above: The wreck of the Ruth Hickman (Halifax, Nova Scotia) which went aground near Searach after her rudder was damaged. The ship was brought to Dingle for repairs and her cargo of yellow meal was sold off. Repairs were carried out but the owners lost interest and she never left Dingle. (photo: 10/12/21)

Left: Fishing fleet wind-bound in Dingle Harbour.

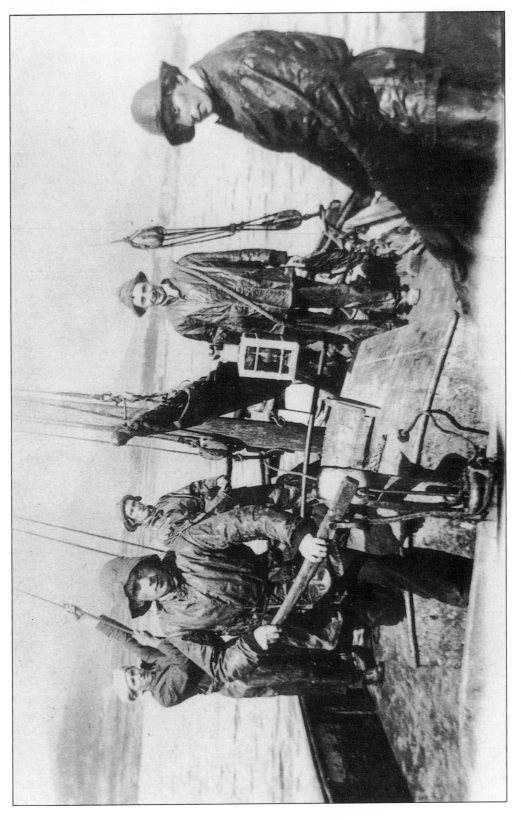

Fishermen in full gear. Front, left to right: John Chipper Long operating pump, Joe Long. Back: Jamie Garvey, Jim Long, Paddy Sullivan.

The Racker Brosnan sitting on 200 lb barrels of Irish mackerel from Dingle. The barrels are stamped with the name Kavanagh – one of Dingle's fish processors. The colony is in the background.

Above: Thady Devane's punt at Reenbeg, March 1925. Left to right: Paddy Long (Joe), Tom Devane (Thady), Paddy Long (Jack), Tom Devane (Tom), Jim Fitzgerald, John Long (Jack), Joe Long (Jack), Jamie Garvey, Paddy Sullivan (Bun). (photo: Maurice McKenna)

Right: Baskets of fish for sale outside Patrick Sheehy's.

The cargo of coal from the ship is loaded on horse and carts to be transferred to storage areas in the town. (1923/24)

Steamboat at the pier.

The pier laden with imported goods. Salt and baskets for the herring trade, and containers of distilled water.

Three-masted schooner with timber at the pier.

Sailboat in Dingle harbour.

The pier is black with people for the annual Blessing of the Boats. The boats are decked out with bunting and flags. (photo: Mikey Quirke)

Barking the nets prior to mackerel fishing. The nets were dragged through a solution of cutch and then left to dry. This process strengthed the nets. Mickey Gerard Brosnan (on left), Louis Graham with pole, Michín Flannery pulling the net, Tom Flannery with cap. 1947. (photo: J. Graham)

The army band leads the parade for the Blessing of the Boats.

Fishermen parade to the pier for the Blessing of the Boats. (photo: Josephine Graham)

Altarboys lead Canon Lyne and the fishermen to the pier. (photo: Josephine Graham)

Above: Canon Lyne blessing the boats.

Left: Tim Brosnan holds a blessed banner during the Blessing of the Boats in the St Laurence O'Toole (John Brosnan, owner).

Below: Rosbeg D101 (Mikey Graham, owner) fully laden for the Blessing of the Boats.

Dingle Nobbies (right to left): Elsie Mabel, D174 (Paddy "waistcoat" Brosnan); Pride of Dingle (Tadhg Flaherty – Red Mike) John Anthony (John Graham), The Pedro (Tommy Devane).

Elsie Mabel D174, the finest boat in Dingle in her time, Jan. 1945. (photo: Murtagh Burke)

Punts on the slip at Dingle Pier. The punts were used to get to and from the boats which were moored out in the harbour. Mikey and Paul Flannery on the right.

Fishing in the Rosdubh (Paddy Bawn's boat) were, left to right, Francie Lovett, Paddy Bawn Brosnan, Tim Brosnan, Tim Devane.

Above: Group on pier, left to right: Paddy Devane, Jimmy McKenna, Bishop Moynihan, Joe Walsh, Michael Kane, Sean Brosnan, Patrick "waistcoat" Brosnan, Paddy Garvey, Joe Flaherty.

Left: Jeanette S074.

The wreck of Naomh Colum (Patrick Flannery) is in the foreground. Moored outside are, left to right: Madonna (Jim Quinn/Mike Walsh), Manx Girl (Dinny Garvey), Majestic (Patsy Flaherty), The Brendan (Joe Flaherty), Laurence O'Toole (Mikey Brosnan), Pride of Kerry (Mikey Flannery), Pride of Ventry (Patrick Curran) Peadar (Tommy Flaherty). (photo: Glynn Davies, Wales)

At high tide the boats would be brought as near to shore as possible so that when the tide went out they were left high and dry. This facilitated painting and repair works that had to be done to the boats. Good Friday was the traditional day for this – the pubs were closed. Boats are, left to right: D184 (unknown), Rosglas (Meado), D167 Diarmuid (Paddy Griffin), Laurence O'Toole (Mikey Brosnan). (photo: J.C. Houlihan)

Above: Denis Murphy changing the wet batteries in Houlihan's powerhouse. A turbine is in the background.

Left: J.C. Houlihan, Dingle businessman.

Left: Paddy Baker and the water wheel at Milltown, and below, at work in the sawmill. The water wheel finally stopped in 1978.

The beginning of great change in Dingle came when the old coastguard station was knocked to build the Skellig Hotel. Standing by the bulldozer are John and Veronica Houlihan.
(photo: V. Houlihan 1968)

Sources of photographs and Information

Where the photographer is known their name appears with the caption. The following people – all from Dingle unless otherwise stated – provided the photos. The name of each source is followed by the number of the page on which the photo appears, plus its position, i.e. T = top, B = bottom, L = left, R = right.

John Ashe, Spa Road, 67T, 131B; Kate Ashe, 33B, 57B, 75R, 94, 118B, 126B, 127B, 128T, 129; Mick Boland, 40B, 44, 95B; Paddy Bawn Brosnan, 41B, 151B; Murtagh Burke, Limerick, 13B, 16B, 58T, 72B, 78, 86B, 150B; Ciarán Cleary, 10T; Eileen T. Cremin, 91, 92, 103B; Owen Curley, Monaghan, 22B, 117, 118T, 146; Gerry Curran, 32, 79; James Curran, 10B; Joe Curran, 125T; Maureen Curran, 113B; Noreen Curran, 17B, 33T, 45, 59, 67B, 69B, 70B, 72T, 149T; Paudie Curran, 85; Francis Daly, Dunquin, 116T, 149BL; Bridget Devane, 135T; Tommy Devane, 11T, 24T, 74B, 152T; Eileen Dillon, 88T, 137T; May Dillon, 22T, 96; David Donegan, 39, 152B; Department of Irish Folklore, UCD, 36T, 40T, 65, 66, 69T, 103T, 127T; Tommy Devane Snr, 58B, 143T; Jimmy Falvey, 134T, 136B; Patsy Fenton, 71, 93T; Kathleen Ferriter, England, 61T; Kitty Flaherty, 156T; Peter Flannery, 115B, 116B; John Joe Fox, 100T; Fox's, 8, 12, 19T, 20, 21, 23, 26T, 31T, 37, 38, 46, 49T, 50, 51, 52B, 53, 54, 64T, 68, 73, 75L, 76, 77B, 88B, 89, 90, 97T, 98, 100B, 102, 105T, 123, 124, 126T, 132, 134B, 137B, 138, 139T, 140B, 144B, 145, 153; Bernie Goggin, 62, 150T; Helen Graham, 149BR; Josephine Graham, 147T, 148; Helen & Ita Griffin, 9, 14B, 83, 86T; John Guiheen, 93B; Josephine Hanlon, 27; Denis Houlihan, 82T, 130T; Vincent Houlihan, 121, 136T, 154, 155, 157; Antoinette Long, 81; Bridie Long, 26BL, 41T, 43T, 48, 49B, 52T, 63, 99B, 119; Lily Lundon, 16TR; Tom Lundon, 64B, 130B; Mrs Lynch, Clonkeen, 56, 87T, 105B, 114, 133B; Ita McCarthy, 57T; Oliver McDonald, 144T; Ita McGrath, Ventry, 15; Walter McGrath, Cork, 24B, 28; Canon Jack McKenna, 16TL, 17TL, 18, 19B nathan Moriarty,

158

34; John Murphy, 140T; Ellen Nelligan, 70T; Eibhlín Ní Shé, Dúnchaoin, 17TR, 21B, 87B, 101B; Liz Nolan, Cork, 13T, 35B; Bridie O'Connor, 18TL, 35T, 36B, 125B, 151T; Hannah O'Connor, Annascaul, 61B, 135B; Michael O'Connor, 104; Nora O'Connor, 60B; Lelia O'Flaherty, Dublin, 31B; Fergus Ó Flaithbheartaigh, 115T, 139B; Cecila O'Shea, 43B, 47; Eileen O'Shea, 42, 120B; Michael F. O'Sullivan, 80; Donal O'Connor, 82B; Brendan Quirke, Medford, USA, 55; Michael Reen, 95T; D.G. Rowlands, England, 25, 29, 84T, 106–111, 113T; Bridie Sheehy, 11B; Jean Sheehy, 14T, 60T, 74T, 77T, 84B, 141, 142, 143B, 147B; Kathleen Thompson, 122, 131T; George Twist, 112, 128B, 156B.

The following provided me with information and/or photographs which I did not have the space to use.

Kate & Thomas Ashe, John Ashe, American Museum of Natural History (Debra L. Baida), Paddy Bawn Brosnan, Evelyn Bambury, Mick Boland, James Brosnan, Jo Anne Barrett, Mrs P. Barrett, Murtagh Burke, Toosie Cotter, Eileen & Tim Collins, James Curran, Noreen Curran, Joe Curran, Maureen Curran, Ciarán Cleary, Eileen T. Cremin, Gerry Curran, Tommy & Bridie Devane, Tommy & Thérèse Devane, David Donegan, Madge Donoghue, Eileen Dillon, Bridget Devane, Fergus Flaherty, Jimmy & Patsy Fenton, James & Peggy Flahive, Peter Flannery, Jimmy & Mikey Falvey, Vincent Flannery, John Guiheen, Josephine Graham, Helen Graham, Danny Graham, Helen & Ita Griffin, Vincent Houlihan, Denis Houlihan, Mikey Houlihan, Noel Kissane (National Library), Tom & Lily Lundon, Bridie Long, Mrs Lynch Clonkeen, Ita McCarthy, Walter McGrath, Oliver McDonald, Canon Jack McKenna, John McSweeney, John Murphy, Patrick Moriarty, Ita McGrath, Jonathan Moriarty, Liz Nolan, Ellen Nelligan, Ríonach Uí Ógáin (Dept of Irish Folklore), Alex O'Donnell, Eileen O'Shea, John "Diony" O'Connor, Jim & Vera O'Keeffe, Michael O'Connor, D.G. Rowlands, Mikey Reen, Liam Reilly, Alice Sullivan, Jean Sheehy, Bridie Sheehy, John & Celeste Slye, Eileen Ní Shé, Cecila Shea, Kathleen Thompson, George Twist, John Joe Murphy, Jimmy McKenna, Stevie Kelliher, Kitty Moriarty, Martin and Bob Rohan.

AIB Bank sponsored my promotional leaflet.

Photographic Notes

The photographs were copied using Kodak Plus X and Kodak T. Max 35mm films. The cameras used were Nikon FE2 and F301 with Nikkor 55mm micro lens and Nikkor 105mm lens with PK13 close-up ring. Many of the weaker photos were copied on a Rollei 6 x 6 which greatly reduced fall-off when enlarging.

Tim McCarthy of Cork was responsible for the majority of the developing and printing of the 35mm films at the early stage. This was the time I was busy collecting the photos and the collecting would not have proceeded as fast as it did if I had had to concentrate on developing and printing.

The Nikkor 55mm micro lens used belongs to Tim and is an ideal lens for this work. Photographs of all sizes can be copied using this lens. Tim also gained access to a Rollei 6 x 6 large format camera, with 80mm lens which has a built-in extension bellows for close-up work. Over half of the photographs in the book were printed by Tim.

Tim's camera equipment, the camera equipment he borrowed, his time and effort played a large part in this project.

Dingle's oldest photo (page 9) was produced using a Ferro type process (Tintype). The print was made in the camera on black or chocolate enamelled tin plates and developed in an iron developer. The process was introduced in 1852 and was very popular due to quick drying times.

As there was no negative involved and the original image was converted into a positive image, it is reversed from left to right – a fact which was rarely pointed out to the customers.